Longman Young Children's Picture Dictionary

PEARSON
Longman

with songs and chants by
Carolyn Graham

Published by
Pearson Longman Asia ELT
20/F Cornwall House
Taikoo Place
979 King's Road
Quarry Bay
Hong Kong

fax: +852 2856 9578
email: pearsonlongman@pearsoned.com.hk
www.longman.com

and Associated Companies throughout the world.

First published 2007
Reprinted 2007 (five times)

Produced by Pearson Education Asia Limited, Hong Kong
EPC/06

ISBN-13: 978-962-00-5410-5
ISBN-10: 962-00-5410-5

Publisher: Simon Campbell
Editor: Angela Cheung
Designers: Junko Funaki, Myth Wong
Illustrators: K.Y. Chan, Tammy Kay, Chris Lensch, Heidi Ma, Bernd Wong, Marco Yip, Eva Yue
Musical Composer: Carolyn Graham
Musical Arranger: Joseph Mennonna
Audio Producer: Eileen Stevens, Full House Productions
Audio Engineer: Matt Verzola, Full House Productions
Voice Artists: Evan Crommett, Lauren Dennis, Struan Erlenborn, Gabby Piacentile, Sally Woodson

We would like to thank © Dorling Kindersley for the mouse photo on p. 28, the cow photo on p. 28 (Geoff Brightling), the sheep photo on p. 28 (Gordon Clayton) and the chicken photo on p. 29 (Mike Dunning). We would like to thank © Jean-Claude Outrequin for the horse photo on p. 28. We would also like to thank Ivanna Wolfinbarger, Emma Gutierrez and Yanis Kwong.

Project Developer
Karen Jamieson

Reviewers
Devon Thagard
Keiko-Abe Ford

We would also like to thank all the teachers who gave feedback and comments on this project.

Contents

Introduction

The **Longman Young Children's Picture Dictionary** has been designed specifically for children aged 2–5 and can be used both in the classroom and at home.

The 270+ words featured in the dictionary have been chosen to help young learners describe the world as they see it. Words are presented in context through 26 age-appropriate topics with engaging songs and chants and simple child-centered dialogs.

The dictionary is accompanied by the **Activity Resource Book** which includes 52 graded activity sheets, photocopiable flashcards and illustrated song and chant actions.

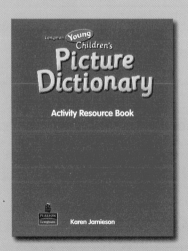

How to use the dictionary

 1 ### The topic

- Before looking at the scene, talk briefly about the topic (in the children's first language if necessary) and ask if they know any English words related to this topic.
- Let the children point and say the words for objects they recognize.

13 In the Kitchen

32

② The vocabulary

- Play the CD and have the children point to each object in the scene.
- Play the CD again and have the children point to the words.

③ The hidden object

- Ask the children to look for the hidden object and then say the word when they find it.

④ The dialog

- Play the CD and have the children listen to the dialog.
- Play the CD again and have the children repeat the dialog along with the CD.
- Have the children practice the dialog with you, taking turns to say part A or part B.

⑤ The song or chant

- Play the CD and have the children listen to the song or chant.
- Play the CD again and have the children point to the objects they hear in the song or chant.
- Break the song or chant into small sections and have the children practice.
- Play the CD and have the children sing along.

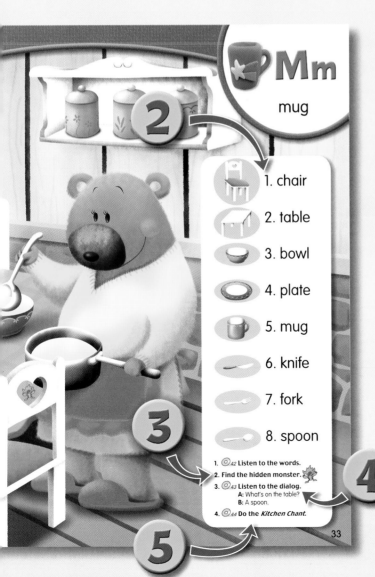

Mm
mug

1. chair
2. table
3. bowl
4. plate
5. mug
6. knife
7. fork
8. spoon

1. 🔘42 **Listen to the words.**
2. **Find the hidden monster.** 🍁
3. 🔘43 **Listen to the dialog.**
   A: What's on the table?
   B: A spoon.
4. 🔘44 **Do the** *Kitchen Chant*.

33

Alphabet

A a 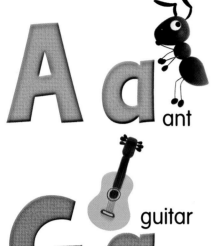 ant

B b  banana

C c  cat

G g  guitar

H h  horse

I i  ice cream

M m  monster

N n  notebook

O o  octopus

S s  sun

T t 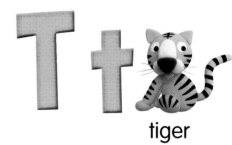 tiger

U u  umbrella

Y y 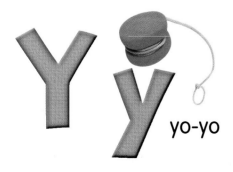 yo-yo

Z z  zebra

D d dog

E e elephant

F f fish

J j jellyfish

K k kite

L l ladybug

P p pen

Q q queen

R r rocket

V v van

W w watch

X x fox

- ◎1 Sing the *Hello Song*.
- ◎2 Sing the *Goodbye Song*.

1. ◎3 Listen to the alphabet.

2. ◎4 Listen to the dialog.
   A: How do you spell "cat?"
   B: C-a-t. Cat.

3. ◎5 Sing the *Alphabet Song*.

3. soda pop

2. candy

1. cake

4. popcorn

Aa

apple

5. apple

6. chips

7. cookies

8. sandwiches

1. ⊚6 **Listen to the words.**
2. **Find the hidden ant.**
3. ⊚7 **Listen to the dialog.**
   A: More, please.
   B: Here you are.
4. ⊚8 **Sing the** *Picnic Song*.

Bugs in the Forest

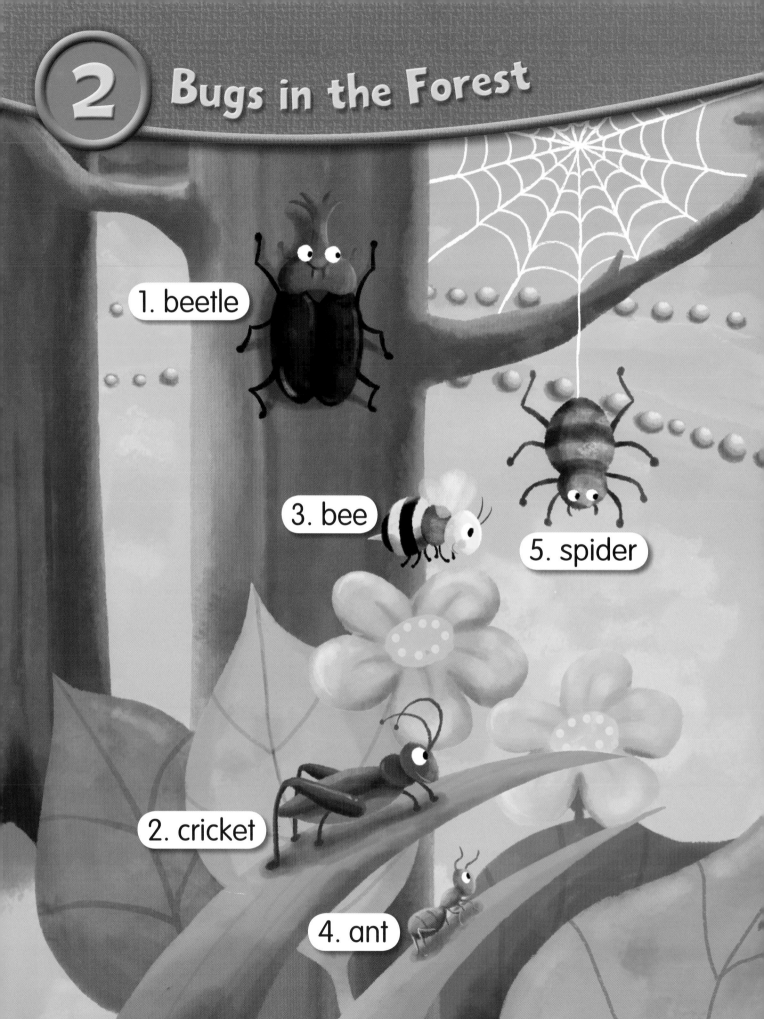

1. beetle

3. bee

5. spider

2. cricket

4. ant

Bb

bee

9. butterfly

6. worm

8. ladybug

7. caterpillar

1. 🎧9 Listen to the words.
2. Find the hidden banana. 🍌
3. 🎧10 Listen to the dialog.
   A: Look! A butterfly!
   B: Wow!
4. 🎧11 Sing the *Bug Song*.

11

1. banana

2. plum

3. peach

4. pear

5. orange

6. coconut

7. pineapple

8. grapes

9. strawberries

1. 🔘12 Listen to the words.

2. Find the hidden cat.

3. 🔘13 Listen to the dialog.
   A: Are you hungry?
   B: Yes. / No.

4. 🔘14 Do the *Fruit Chant*.

coconut

3. sun

5. cloud

1. tree

4. yard

2. grass

6. sky

Dd
door

9. house

7. door

8. window

10. flower

1. 🔘15 **Listen to the words.**
2. **Find the hidden dog.**
3. 🔘16 **Listen to the dialog.**
   A: I can see the house.
   B: Me, too!
4. 🔘17 **Sing the *Outdoors Song*.**

15

 1. head

 2. ears

 3. eyes

 4. nose

 5. mouth

 6. arm

 7. elbow

 8. hand

 9. leg

 10. foot

1. 18 **Listen to the words.**
2. **Find the hidden elephant.**
3. 19 **Listen to the dialog.**
   A: Touch your ears.
   B: OK.
4. 20 **Sing the *Body Song*.**

Ee

elbow

F f

family

 1. mommy

 2. daddy

 3. brother

 4. sister

 5. baby sister

 6. grandpa

 7. grandma

 8. family

1. ⊚21 Listen to the words.
2. **Find the hidden fish.**
3. ⊚22 **Listen to the dialog.**
   A: Who's that?
   B: My brother.
4. ⊚23 **Sing the** *Family Song.*

1. girl

3. pencil

2. paper

4. scissors

5. glue

Gg girl

6. teacher

8. boy

9. pen

7. notebook

Sarah

Joe

1. ⊚24 Listen to the words.
2. Find the hidden guitar.
3. ⊚25 Listen to the dialog.
   A: Pass the glue, please.
   B: Here you are.
4. ⊚26 Sing the *Classroom Song.*

8 Shape Town

1. pink

2. brown

3. orange

4. green

5. purple

6. heart

7. square

8. circle

9. triangle

10. rectangle

1. 27 **Listen to the words.**

2. **Find the hidden horse.**

3. ⊙28 **Listen to the dialog.**
   A: Draw a circle. Color it pink!
   B: OK.

4. ⊙29 **Sing the *Shape Song*.**

22

Hh

heart

23

9 Painting a Picture

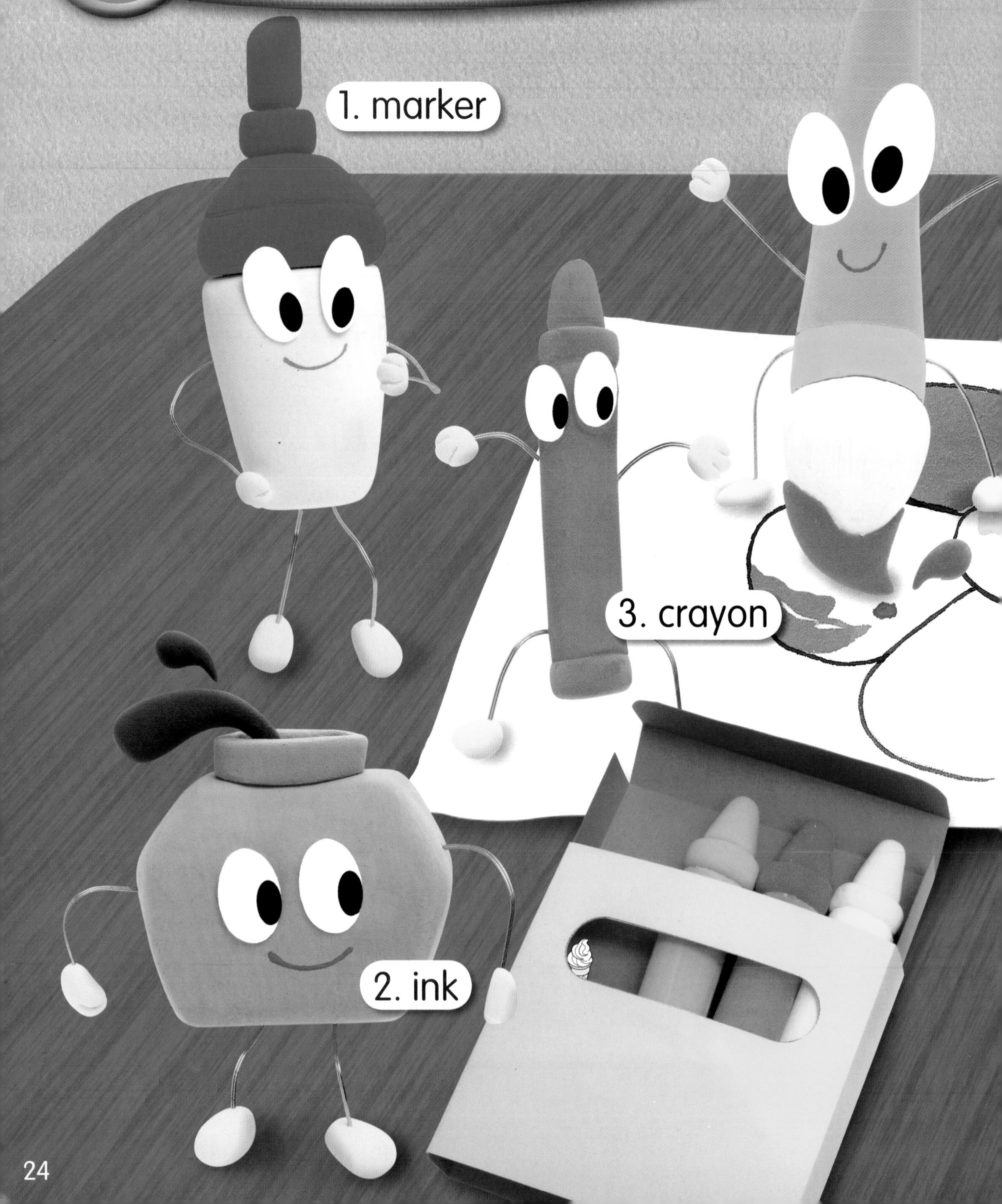

1. marker

2. ink

3. crayon

24

ink **Ii**

5. brush

6. red

7. yellow

8. blue

9. white

10. black

4. paint

1. 30 **Listen to the words.**

2. **Find the hidden ice cream.**

3. 31 **Listen to the dialog.**
   A: Look at the crayon.
   B: It's red.

4. 32 **Do the** *Picture Chant.*

25

3. kite

1. jungle gym

4. jump rope

2. sandbox

J j

jump rope

8. swing

5. seesaw

6. ball

7. slide

1. 🎧33 Listen to the words.
2. Find the hidden jellyfish.
3. 🎧34 Listen to the dialog.
   A: Let's play!
   B: OK.
4. 🎧35 Sing the *Park Song*.

1. cow

2. sheep

3. mouse

4. dog

5. puppy

Kk

kitten

6. horse

7. cat

8. kitten

9. chicken

10. rabbit

1. 🎧36 **Listen to the words.**
2. **Find the hidden kite.**
3. 🎧37 **Listen to the dialog.**
   A: Hey, what's that?
   B: It's a mouse.
4. 🎧38 **Do the** *Zoo Chant*.

1. carrot

2. broccoli

3. tomato

4. cabbage

5. potato

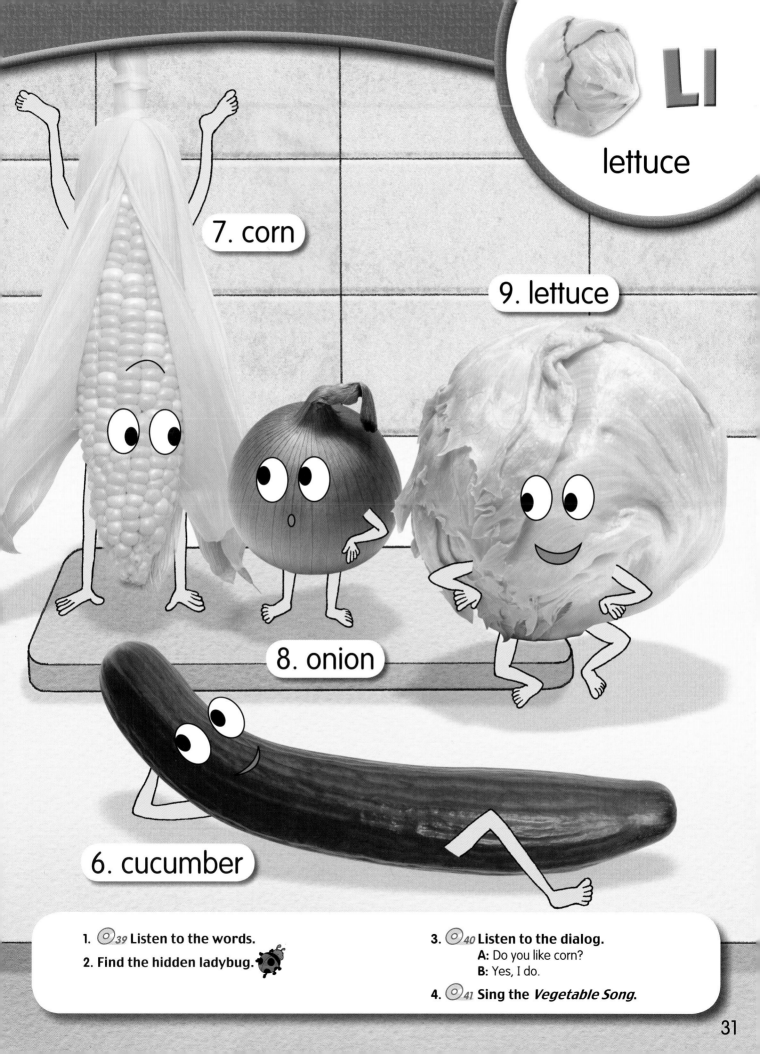

Ll

lettuce

7. corn

9. lettuce

8. onion

6. cucumber

1. ◎39 **Listen to the words.**

2. **Find the hidden ladybug.**

3. ◎40 **Listen to the dialog.**
   A: Do you like corn?
   B: Yes, I do.

4. ◎41 **Sing the *Vegetable Song*.**

Mm

mug

1. chair
2. table
3. bowl
4. plate
5. mug
6. knife
7. fork
8. spoon

1. 🔘42 **Listen to the words.**
2. **Find the hidden monster.**
3. 🔘43 **Listen to the dialog.**
   A: What's on the table?
   B: A spoon.
4. 🔘44 **Do the Kitchen Chant.**

33

1. hat

 2. scarf

 3. gloves

 4. necklace

 5. jacket

 6. sweatshirt

 7. pants

 8. sneakers

 9. shoes

 10. boots

1. ⊙45 **Listen to the words.**

2. **Find the hidden notebook.**

3. ⊙46 **Listen to the dialog.**
   A: It's cold.
   B: Put on your scarf.

4. ⊙47 **Do the *Clothes Chant*.**

Nn

necklace

1. milk

2. porridge

3. sugar

4. coffee

5. bread

1. 🔘48 Listen to the words.

2. Find the hidden octopus.

3. 🔘49 Listen to the dialog.
   A: Orange juice?
   B: Yes, please. / No, thanks.

4. 🔘50 Do the *Breakfast Chant*.

orange
juice

6. butter

8. orange juice

7. cheese

37

The Living Room

3. picture

1. TV

4. bookcase

2. armchair

5. book

6. clock

Pp

picture

8. sofa

7. telephone

1. 🔘51 Listen to the words.
2. Find the hidden pen. ✏️
3. 🔘52 Listen to the dialog.
   A: Where's the book?
   B: There!
4. 🔘53 Do the *Living Room Chant*.

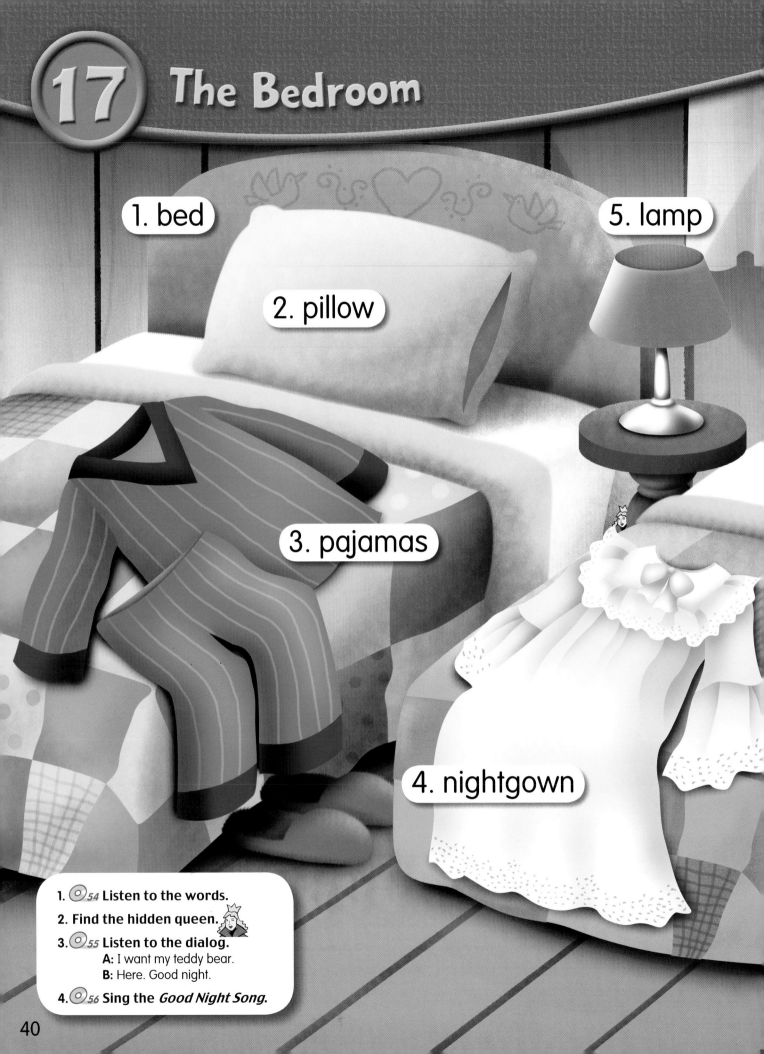

17 The Bedroom

1. bed

2. pillow

3. pajamas

4. nightgown

5. lamp

1. 🎧54 **Listen to the words.**

2. **Find the hidden queen.**

3. 🎧55 **Listen to the dialog.**
   A: I want my teddy bear.
   B: Here. Good night.

4. 🎧56 **Sing the** *Good Night Song.*

Qq

quilt

6. quilt

7. teddy bear

8. slippers

41

1. polar bear

2. seal

3. Santa

Rr

reindeer

7. presents

4. sleigh

8. reindeer

5. elves

9. snowman

6. penguin

1. ⊚57 Listen to the words.

2. Find the hidden rocket.

3. ⊚58 Listen to the dialog.
   A: Merry Christmas!
   B: Happy Holidays!

4. ⊚59 Sing the *Christmas Song*.

1. doll

3. monster

2. bike

4. violin

Ss

snake

5. snake

8. monkey

7. fox

9. guitar

6. drum

1. 🔘60 **Listen to the words.**

2. **Find the hidden sun.** ☀

3. 🔘61 **Listen to the dialog.**
   A: What's that?
   B: A drum.

4. 🔘62 **Do the** *Toy Chant*.

45

The Bathroom

3. hairbrush

1. towel

2. toilet

toothbrush

4. shower

9. mirror

5. soap

10. sink

7. toothbrush

6. bathtub

8. toothpaste

1. ○63 **Listen to the words.**
2. **Find the hidden tiger.**
3. ○64 **Listen to the dialog.**
   A: Get ready for bed!
   B: OK.
4. ○65 **Do the *Bathroom Chant*.**

1. shirt

 2. T-shirt

 3. dress

 4. skirt

 5. shorts

 6. sandals

 7. swimsuit

 8. sunglasses

 9. watch

 10. umbrella

1. ⊚66 **Listen to the words.**

2. **Find the hidden umbrella.**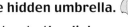

3. ⊚67 **Listen to the dialog.**
   A: Put on your sandals.
   B: OK.

4. ⊚68 **Sing the** *Sunny Day Song*.

Uu
umbrella

 1. chicken

 2. fish

 3. steak

 4. rice

 5. noodles

 6. vegetables

 7. water

 8. tea

1. ◎69 **Listen to the words.**
2. **Find the hidden van.**
3. ◎70 **Listen to the dialog.**
   A: I like steak.
   B: Me, too! / Not me. I like chicken.
4. ◎71 **Do the *Dinner Chant*.**

V v
vegetables

51

1. shark

2. jellyfish

3. fish

4. seahorse

5. whale

W w

whale

9. turtle

8. dolphin

6. crab

10. octopus

7. starfish

1. ⊚72 **Listen to the words.**
2. **Find the hidden watch.**
3. ⊚73 **Listen to the dialog.**
   A: Look at the starfish!
   B: Wow!
4. ⊚74 **Sing the** *Underwater Song.*

53

1. box

2. yo-yo

3. van

4. car

5. rocket

1. ⊙75 **Listen to the words.**
2. **Find the hidden fox.**
3. ⊙76 **Listen to the dialog.**
   A: Let's play with the car.
   B: OK.
4. ⊙77 **Do the** *Playtime Chant*.

6. plane

box

Xx

9. train

7. bus

8. boat

10. truck

55

1. hamburger

3. soup

4. salad

2. ice cream

Yy
yogurt

5. hot dog

7. yogurt

6. sausages

9. eggs

8. fries

1. ⊙78 **Listen to the words.**

2. **Find the hidden yo-yo.**

3. ⊙79 **Listen to the dialog.**
A: Are you hungry?
B: Yes.
A: Here you are.
B: Thank you.

4. ⊙80 **Do the** *Restaurant Chant.*

1. bird

2. lion

3. kangaroo

4. giraffe

1. ◎81 **Listen to the words.**
2. **Find the hidden zebra.**
3. ◎82 **Listen to the dialog.**
   A: What am I?
   B: A kangaroo!
   A: No. Try again!
4. ◎83 **Do the *Animal Chant*.**

Zz

zebra

5. gorilla

8. tiger

9. crocodile

6. hippo

7. zebra

10. elephant

59

1. queen

2. prince

3. Snow White

4. dwarves

1 one

2 two

1. ⊚84 **Listen to the words.**
2. ⊚85 **Listen to the numbers.**
3. ⊚86 **Listen to the dialog.**
   A: How old are you?
   B: I'm 4!

3 three

4 four

5 five

6 six

7 seven

8 eight

9 nine

10 ten

Bonus 2 Adjectives

1. happy
2. sad
3. sleepy
4. hungry
5. thirsty

I'm ...

1. ⊙87 **Listen to the adjectives.**

2. ⊙88 **Listen to the dialog.**
A: How do you feel?
B: I'm sleepy.

3. ⊙89 **Listen to the dialog.**
A: What's it like?
B: It's yummy.

It's ...

6. big

7. small

8. scary

9. yucky

10. yummy

1. sunny

2. windy

3. cloudy

4. rainy

1. 🎧90 **Listen to the words.**

2. 🎧91 **Listen to the dialog.**
A: What's the weather like?
B: It's sunny!

5. cold

6. hot

7. warm

8. cool

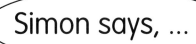

Simon says, ...

1. touch your nose

2. rub your tummy

3. shake your hands

1. ◎92 **Listen to the actions.**
2. ◎93 **Listen to the dialog.**
   A: Simon says, "Run!"
   A: Simon says, "Jump!"

4. stand up

5. jump

6. run

7. walk

8. hop

9. sit down

Alphabetical Word List

A

ant	6–7
	10–11
apple	8–9
arm	16–17
armchair	38–39

B

baby sister	18–19
ball	26–27
banana	6–7
	12–13
bathtub	46–47
bed	40–41
bee	10–11
beetle	10–11
big	62–63
bike	44–45
bird	58–59
black	24–25
blue	24–25
boat	54–55
book	38–39
bookcase	38–39
boots	34–35
bowl	32–33
box	54–55
boy	20–21
bread	36–37
broccoli	30–31
brother	18–19
brown	22–23
brush	24–25
bus	54–55
butter	36–37
butterfly	10–11

C

cabbage	30–31
cake	8–9
candy	8–9
car	54–55
carrot	30–31
cat	6–7
	28–29
caterpillar	10–11

chair	32–33
cheese	36–37
chicken (bird)	28–29
chicken (food)	50–51
chips	8–9
circle	22–23
clock	38–39
cloud	14–15
cloudy	64–65
coconut	12–13
coffee	36–37
cold	64–65
cookies	8–9
cool	64–65
corn	30–31
cow	28–29
crab	52–53
crayon	24–25
cricket	10–11
crocodile	58–59
cucumber	30–31

D

daddy	18–19
dog	6–7
	28–29
doll	44–45
dolphin	52–53
door	14–15
dress	48–49
drum	44–45
dwarves	60–61

E

ears	16–17
eggs	56–57
eight	60–61
elbow	16–17
elephant	6–7
	58–59
elves	42–43
eyes	16–17

F

family	18–19
fish (animal)	6–7
	52–53

fish (food)	50–51
five	60–61
flower	14–15
foot	16–17
fork	32–33
four	60–61
fox	6–7
	44–45
fries	56–57

G

giraffe	58–59
girl	20–21
gloves	34–35
glue	20–21
gorilla	58–59
grandma	18–19
grandpa	18–19
grapes	12–13
grass	14–15
green	22–23
guitar	6–7
	44–45

H

hairbrush	46–47
hamburger	56–57
hand	16–17
happy	62–63
hat	34–35
head	16–17
heart	22–23
hippo	58–59
hop	66–67
horse	6–7
	28–29
hot	64–65
hot dog	56–57
house	14–15
hungry	62–63

I

ice cream	6–7
	56–57
ink	24–25

J

jacket	34–35
jellyfish	6–7
	52–53
jump	66–67
jump rope	26–27
jungle gym	26–27

K

kangaroo	58–59
kite	6–7
	26–27
kitten	28–29
knife	32–33

L

ladybug	6–7
	10–11
lamp	40–41
leg	16–17
lettuce	30–31
lion	58–59

M

marker	24–25
milk	36–37
mirror	46–47
mommy	18–19
monkey	44–45
monster	6–7
	44–45
mouse	28–29
mouth	16–17
mug	32–33

N

necklace	34–35
nightgown	40–41
nine	60–61
noodles	50–51
nose	16–17
notebook	6–7
	20–21

Thematic Word List

Actions

Bonus Topic 4 pp. 66–67
hop
jump
rub your tummy
run
shake your hands
sit down
stand up
touch your nose
walk

Adjectives

Bonus Topic 2 pp. 62–63
big
happy
hungry
sad
scary
sleepy
small
thirsty
yucky
yummy

Bonus Topic 3 pp. 64–65
cloudy
cold
cool
hot
rainy
sunny
warm
windy

Animals

Topic 2   pp. 10–11
ant
bee
beetle
butterfly
caterpillar
cricket
ladybug

spider
worm

Topic 11   pp. 28–29
cat
chicken
cow
dog
horse
kitten
mouse
puppy
rabbit
sheep

Topic 18   pp. 42–43
penguin
polar bear
reindeer
seal

Topic 19   pp. 44–45
fox
monkey
snake

Topic 23   pp. 52–53
crab
dolphin
fish
jellyfish
octopus
seahorse
shark
starfish
turtle
whale

Topic 26   pp. 58–59
bird
crocodile
elephant
giraffe
gorilla
hippo
kangaroo
lion
tiger
zebra

Clothing and Accessories

Topic 14   pp. 34–35
boots
gloves
hat
jacket
necklace
pants
scarf
shoes
sneakers
sweatshirt

Topic 17   pp. 40–41
nightgown
pajamas
slippers

Topic 21   pp. 48–49
dress
sandals
shirt
shorts
skirt
sunglasses
swimsuit
T-shirt
umbrella
watch

Colors, Numbers and Shapes

Topic 8   pp. 22–23
brown
circle
green
heart
orange
pink
purple
rectangle
square
triangle

Topic 9   pp. 24–25
black
blue
red
white
yellow

Bonus Topic 1 pp. 60–61
one
two
three
four
five
six
seven
eight
nine
ten

Food and Drink

Topic 1   pp. 8–9
cake
candy
chips
cookies
popcorn
sandwiches
soda pop

Topic 15   pp. 36–37
bread
butter
cheese
coffee
milk
orange juice
porridge
sugar

Topic 22   pp. 50–51
chicken
fish
noodles
rice
steak
tea
water

Topic 25   pp. 56–57
eggs
fries
hamburger
hot dog
ice cream
salad
sausages
soup
yogurt

Songs and Chants

Alphabet
pp. 6–7

 **Hello Song**

Hello Harry, Hello, Hello
Hello Mary, Hello, Hello
Hello Sandy, Hello Andy
Hello Joe, Hello.

Hello Freddy, Hello, Hello
Hello Teddy, Hello, Hello
Hello Sally, Hello Anne
Hello Joe, Hello.

[Karaoke version]

 Goodbye Song

Bye-bye Harry, Goodbye, Goodbye
Bye-bye Mary, Goodbye, Goodbye
Bye-bye Sandy, Bye-bye Andy
Bye-bye Joe, Goodbye.

Bye-bye Freddy, Goodbye, Goodbye
Bye-bye Teddy, Goodbye, Goodbye
Bye-bye Sally, Bye-bye Anne
Bye-bye Joe, Goodbye.

[Karaoke version]

5 Alphabet Song

A, B, C, D, E, F, G
H, I, J, K
L, M, N, O, P

Q, R, S, T, U, V
W, W, W, W
X, Y, Z

Topic 1
pp. 8–9

8 Picnic Song

Cookies, sandwich
Soda pop, soda pop
Cookies, popcorn, candy

More popcorn, more soda pop
More candy, please.

Popcorn, candy
Here you are!

Apple, candy
Here you are!

Cookies, sandwich
Here you are!

More popcorn, please.

Topic 2
pp. 10–11

 Bug Song

Cricket, spider, butterfly, bee
Cricket, spider, butterfly, bee

Cricket, ladybug
Cricket, butterfly
Cricket, caterpillar. Wow!

Cricket, beetle, butterfly, ant
Cricket, beetle, butterfly, ant
Cricket, beetle
Cricket, butterfly

Look! A butterfly!
Wow!

Topic 3
pp. 12–13

 Fruit Chant

Peach, banana, coconut, pear
Peach, banana, coconut, pear
Peach
Pineapple
Grapes
Strawberries
Peach, banana, coconut, pear

Are you hungry? [CLAP]
Yes! [CLAP]
Are you hungry? [CLAP]
No.

Peach, banana, coconut, pear
Peach, banana, coconut, pear
Orange, plum, pineapple, pear
Orange, plum, pineapple, pear

Are you hungry? [CLAP]
Yes! [CLAP]
Are you hungry? [CLAP]
No.

Topic 4
pp. 14–15

 Outdoors Song

I can see the tree.
Me, too!
Me, too!

I can see the sky.
Me, too!
Me, too!

I can see the grass.
I can see the yard.

I can see the sun.
Me, too!
Me, too!

I can see the flower.
Me, too!

I can see the cloud.
Me, too!
Me, too!

I can see the window.
I can see the door.
I can see the house.
Me, too!
Me, too!

Topic 5
pp. 16–17

20 Body Song

Eyes, ears, nose, mouth
Grandma, is that you?
Eyes, ears, nose, mouth
Grandma, is that you?

Is that you, Grandma?
Yes, it is.
Is that you, Grandma?
Yes, it is.
Touch your eyes.
Touch your ears.
Grandma, is that you?

Arm, leg, elbow, hand
Grandma, is that you?
Arm, leg, elbow, hand
Grandma, is that you?

Touch your arm.
Touch your elbow.
Touch your foot.
Touch your leg.
Touch your eyes.
Touch your ears.

Grandma, is that you?
Yes!

Topic 6
pp. 18–19

 Family Song

Mommy, daddy
Sister, brother
Mommy, daddy
Grandma, grandpa
Mommy, daddy
Baby sister
My family!

Who's that?
My mommy.
Who's that?
My daddy.
Who's that?
My sister.
Who's that?
My brother.
Who's that?
My grandma.
Who's that?
My grandpa.
Who's that?
My baby sister.
That's my family!

Topic 7 pp. 20–21

26 Classroom Song

Pen, pencil
Pen, paper
Scissors, paper, glue
Pen, pencil
Pen, notebook
Scissors, paper, glue

Pass the pen, please.
Here you are.
Pass the pencil, please.
Here you are.

Teacher, girl
Teacher, boy
Pen, pencil, glue
Teacher, girl
Teacher, boy
Pen, pencil, glue

Pass the paper, please.
Here you are.
Pass the notebook, please.
Here you are.

Topic 8 pp. 22–23

29 Shape Song

Circle, heart, square [CLAP]
Circle, heart, square [CLAP]
Triangle
Triangle
Rectangle
Rectangle
Circle, heart, square [CLAP]
Circle, heart, square
Triangle, rectangle, square [CLAP]

Draw a circle. Color it pink!
OK. OK.
Draw a heart. Color it green!
OK. OK.

Draw a square.
Color it purple!
Color it purple!
Color it purple!

Draw a rectangle.
Color it orange!
Draw a triangle.
Color it brown!

Pink circle. Green heart.
Purple square. Purple square.
Orange rectangle. Brown triangle.
Purple, purple, square.
Wow!

Topic 9 pp. 24–25

32 Picture Chant

Brush, marker, crayon, ink
Brush, marker, crayon, ink

Look at the crayon.
[CLAP] It's red.
Look at the marker.
[CLAP] It's blue.
Red crayon.
Blue marker.
Look at my picture.
[CLAP] Good job!

Look at the ink.
[CLAP] It's black.
Look at the paint.
[CLAP] It's yellow.
Black ink.
Yellow paint.
Look at my picture.
[CLAP] Good job!

Topic 10 pp. 26–27

35 Park Song

Seesaw, sandbox, jungle gym
Seesaw, sandbox, jungle gym
Seesaw, jump rope
Seesaw, slide
Seesaw, swing, jungle gym

Kite, ball
Jungle gym
Kite, ball
Jungle gym

Let's play.
OK. Let's play.
Let's play on the jungle gym.
[CLAP, CLAP]

Let's play.
OK. Let's play.
Let's play on the jungle gym.

Topic 11 pp. 28–29

38 Zoo Chant

Cat, kitten
Dog, puppy
Rabbit, mouse, cow [MOO]

Cat, kitten
Dog, puppy
Rabbit, mouse, cow [MOO]

Cat, kitten, horse [NEIGH]
Cat, kitten, sheep [BAA-A-A]

Cat, kitten
Chicken [BOK-BOK-BOK]
Rabbit, mouse, cow [MOO]

Hey, what's that?
It's a horse.
Hey, what's that?
It's a cow.
Hey, what's that?
It's a chicken.
Hey, what's that?
It's a cat. [MEOW]

Topic 12 pp. 30–31

41 Vegetable Song

Cucumber, broccoli
Cucumber, corn
Do you like onions?
Yes, I do.

Cucumber, broccoli
Cucumber, corn
Do you like potatoes?
Yes, I do.

Cucumber, broccoli
Carrots, cabbage
Do you like tomatoes?
Yes, I do.

Onions, potatoes
Lettuce and tomatoes
Do you like broccoli?
Yes, I do.

Topic 13   pp. 32–33

 Kitchen Chant

Table, chair
Table, chair
Knife
Fork
Spoon

Table, chair
Table, chair
Knife
Fork
Spoon

What's on the table?
A spoon.
What's on the table?
A knife.
What's on the table?
A fork, a knife and a spoon.

What's on the table?
A spoon.
What's on the table?
A knife.
What's on the table?
A fork, a knife and a spoon.

Topic 14   pp. 34–35

47 Clothes Chant

Sneakers, sweatshirt
It's cold.
Put on your sweatshirt.
OK.

Pants, jacket
It's cold.
Put on your jacket.
OK.

Boots, hat
It's cold.
Put on your hat.
OK.

Shoes, scarf
It's cold.
Put on your scarf.
OK.

Topic 15   pp. 36–37

50 Breakfast Chant

Orange juice?
Yes, please.
Bread and butter?
No, thanks.
Porridge and milk?
Yes, please.
Sugar?
No, thanks.
Cheese?
Yes, please.
Coffee?
No, thanks.

Topic 16   pp. 38–39

53 Living Room Chant

Where? Where?
Armchair, book
Bookcase, sofa
Where? Where?
Armchair, clock
TV

Where's the telephone?
There! [CLAP]
Where?
There! [CLAP]

Where's the telephone?
There! [CLAP]
Where?
There! [CLAP]

Topic 17   pp. 40–41

 Good Night Song

Bed, pillow, teddy bear, teddy bear
Bed, pillow, teddy bear, teddy bear
Lamp, slippers, quilt, pajamas
I want my teddy bear.

Good night, bed.
Good night, pillow.
Good night, lamp.
Good night, slippers.
Good night, quilt.
Good night, pajamas.
I want my teddy bear.

Here. Good night.

Topic 18   pp. 42–43

 Christmas Song

Reindeer, sleigh, Merry Christmas!
Snowman, elves, Merry Christmas!
Santa, presents, Merry Christmas!
Happy Holidays!
Thanks!

Snowman, polar bear, Merry Christmas!
Penguin, seal, Merry Christmas!
Santa, presents, Merry Christmas!
Happy Holidays!
Thanks!

Topic 19   pp. 44–45

62 Toy Chant

Doll, monkey, fox [CLAP]
Doll, monkey, snake [CLAP]
Doll, monkey, bike [CLAP]
Doll, monkey, monster

Doll, monkey, fox [CLAP]
Doll, monkey, snake [CLAP]
Doll, monkey, bike [CLAP]
Doll, monkey, monster

What's that?
[CLAP] A fox.
What's that?
[CLAP] A drum.
What's that?
[CLAP] A guitar.
What's that?
[CLAP] A violin.

Doll, monkey, fox [CLAP]
Doll, monkey, snake [CLAP]
Doll, monkey, bike [CLAP]
Doll, monkey, monster

Topic 20   pp. 46–47

 Bathroom Chant

Sink, toilet, bathtub, shower
Sink, toilet, bathtub, shower

Hairbrush!
Hairbrush!

Toothbrush!
Toothbrush!

Toothpaste!
Toothpaste!

Get ready for bed!
OK!

Sink, toilet, bathtub, shower
Sink, toilet, bathtub, shower
[CLAP] Get ready for bed!
OK!

Topic 21   pp. 48–49

68 Sunny Day Song

Put on your shorts.
OK!

Put on your T-shirt.
Put on your T-shirt.
Put on your dress.
Put on your skirt.
Put on your shorts.
OK!

Shorts, T-shirt, dress, skirt
Put on your shorts.
OK!

Put on your swimsuit.
OK!
Put on your sandals.
Put on your sandals.

Put on your sunglasses.
Put on your watch.
Put on your shorts.
OK!

Swimsuit, sandals, sunglasses, watch
Put on your shorts.
OK!

Topic 22   pp. 50–51

71 Dinner Chant

I like steak.
[CLAP] Me, too!
I like chicken.
[CLAP] Me, too!
I like fish.
[CLAP] Not me.
I like steak. [CLAP, CLAP]

I like rice.
[CLAP] Me, too!
I like noodles.
[CLAP] Me, too!
I like vegetables.
[CLAP] Not me.
I like steak. [CLAP, CLAP]

Chicken, noodles, fish, rice
Chicken, noodles, fish, rice

I like chicken.
I like noodles.
I like fish.
I like rice.
[CLAP] Not me.
I like steak.

Topic 23   pp. 52–53

74 Underwater Song

Starfish
Jellyfish
Starfish
Octopus
Dolphin, seahorse
Turtle, whale

Starfish, shark
Look at the shark!
Shark! Wow!
Look at the octopus.
Look at the whale.

Starfish
Jellyfish
Starfish
Octopus
Dolphin, seahorse
Turtle, whale

Starfish
Jellyfish
Look at the octopus.
Look at the starfish.
Look at the whale.

Topic 24   pp. 54–55

77 Playtime Chant

Bus, rocket, train
Bus [CLAP], bus [CLAP]
Car, yo-yo, plane
Car [CLAP], car [CLAP]
Bus, rocket, train
Train [CLAP], train [CLAP]
Car, yo-yo, plane
Plane [CLAP], plane [CLAP]

Let's play with the car.
OK.
Let's play with the train.
OK.
Let's play with the bus.
OK.

Let's play with the plane.
OK.

Bus, rocket, train
Bus [CLAP], bus [CLAP]
Car, yo-yo, plane
Car [CLAP], car [CLAP]
Bus, rocket, train
Train [CLAP], train [CLAP]
Car, yo-yo, plane
Plane [CLAP], plane [CLAP]

Topic 25   pp. 56–57

80 Restaurant Chant

Hamburger
Fries
Soup
Salad
Hot dog, hot dog, soup
Wow!

Are you hungry?
Yes! Yes!
Here you are.
Thank you.

Sausages
Eggs
Hot dog
Salad
Yogurt, ice cream, soup
Wow!

Are you hungry?
Yes! Yes!
Here you are.
Thank you.

Topic 26   pp. 58–59

83 Animal Chant

Tiger, elephant, hippo, hippo
Tiger, elephant, bird. Oh!
Zebra, gorilla, crocodile, crocodile
Oh! A kangaroo!

What am I?
A giraffe!
No. Try again!

What am I?
A gorilla!
No. Try again!

What am I?
A kangaroo!
Yes! Good for you!